IS THE BIBLE PERSONALLY FROM GOD?

THE REAL TRUTH
ABOUT LIVING LIKE JESUS

IS THE BIBLE PERSONALLY FROM GOD?

THE REAL TRUTH ABOUT LIVING LIKE JESUS

Younger Children's Workbook
Grades 1-3

JOSH McDOWELL
Dave Bellis
with Cindy Ann Pitts

Is the Bible Personally From God?

Undated Elective Curriculum/Primary (Grades 1 and 2)
Undated Elective Curriculum/Middler (Grades 3 and 4)
Undated Elective Curriculum/Preteen (Grades 5 and 6)

Published by Green Key Books
2514 Aloha Place
Holiday, Florida 34691

Printed in the United States of America

06 07 08 09 / 5 4 3 2 1

IS THE BIBLE PERSONALLY FROM GOD

Table of Contents

WHO WROTE THE BIBLE?

Every Scripture passage is inspired by God. 2 Timothy 3:16

God wants you to get to know him personally. He created you to want to get to know him. He inspired and directed over 40 people to record his message so you could have the Bible to help you know about God and what he is like. The Bible is the world's best selling book.

The Bible is a holy book. The word "holy" means "set apart for" or "by God." There is no other book in the world that can compare to the Bible. We must respect the message the Bible has for us. We need to willingly choose to obey God's words.

> **Big Truth:**
> God personally wrote and directed the writing of his Word the Bible.

Today we will learn about two Bible writers. Moses wrote the first five books in the Old Testament. On Mount Sinai, God gave Moses his laws, which included the Ten Commandments.

John the disciple wrote five New Testament books, including the last book of our Bible, the book of Revelation. ***"I heard a loud voice behind me like a trumpet, saying, 'Write on a scroll what you see, and send it to the seven churches'"*** (Revelation 1:10, 11). John clearly says that the Holy Spirit of God gave him the power to write God's message down.

The Bible was created by God. He inspired over 40 different writers to record his message. Design your own stained glass by coloring in the word INSPIRED written on this Bible. Inspired means "to breathe in."

"Every Scripture passage is inspired by God." 2 Timothy 3:16

I Wrote For God

• I was a Bible writer and a King. • I asked God to give me wisdom. • I was the second son of King David. Who am I? _____ *(See I Kings 3)*	• I am the Bible writer who wrote the first five books of the Bible. • I was born in Egypt. Who am I? _____ *(See Exodus 34:27)*
• I was a doctor when God chose me to be a Bible writer. • I was a friend of Paul's. Who am I? _____ *(See Colossians 4:14)*	• I am a Bible writer who Jesus loved. • Jesus changed my name. • Because of fear, I denied that I knew Jesus three times the night he was arrested. Who am I? _____ *(See Matthew 4:18)*

The WORD Swirl

Begin with the 'e' next to the start in the center of the puzzle and mark out every other letter after the 'e'. After all of the appropriate letters are marked out, use the remaining letters in the blanks below to spell out the verse.

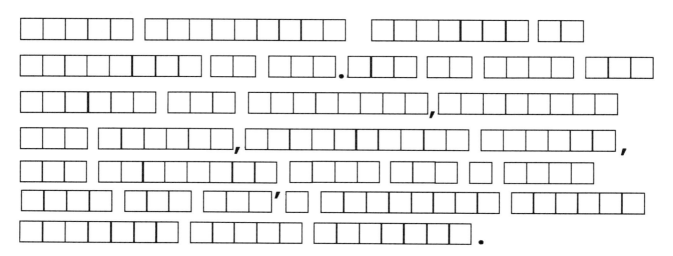

WHY GOD GAVE US THE BIBLE

*This is eternal life: to know You, the only true God,
and Jesus Christ, whom You sent.* John 17:3

God gave us the Bible so that we could get to know him and discover what he is like. The Bible is a one-of-a-kind book; there is none like it anywhere. There are many wonderful books about the Bible, but none of them can take the place of God's holy Word.

In Genesis, the first book of the Bible, we find the story of Adam and Eve, the first two people God created. When God made them, they were perfect. God placed them in a perfect world. He gave them just one rule to obey. They disobeyed God's one rule for them and they sinned. Since then all people have sinned and need God's forgiveness.

> **Big Truth:**
> The Bible is God's way for you to know him so you can be like him.

Jesus provided the forgiveness for our sins that we need. Jesus willingly died on a cross and took the punishment for sin on himself. If we can believe that when Jesus died on the cross he was taking the punishment for our sin and that when he arose from the dead he was proving that he was God and he had the power to forgive our sins, we can ask for forgiveness, and he will forgive us and give us eternal life with him in heaven.

Divisions of the Books of the Bible—Playlist

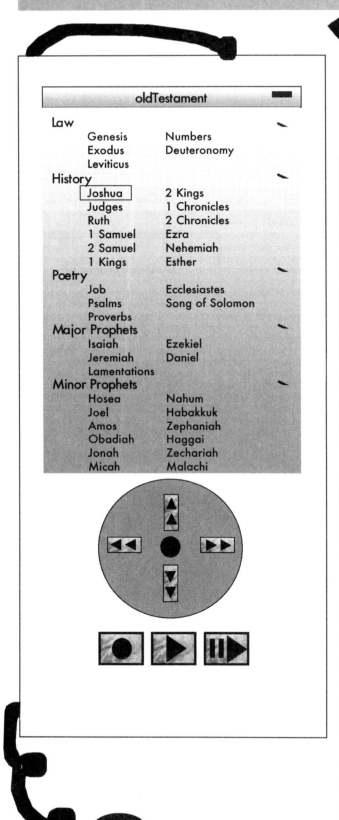

oldTestament

Law
- Genesis
- Exodus
- Leviticus
- Numbers
- Deuteronomy

History
- Joshua
- Judges
- Ruth
- 1 Samuel
- 2 Samuel
- 1 Kings
- 2 Kings
- 1 Chronicles
- 2 Chronicles
- Ezra
- Nehemiah
- Esther

Poetry
- Job
- Psalms
- Proverbs
- Ecclesiastes
- Song of Solomon

Major Prophets
- Isaiah
- Jeremiah
- Lamentations
- Ezekiel
- Daniel

Minor Prophets
- Hosea
- Joel
- Amos
- Obadiah
- Jonah
- Micah
- Nahum
- Habakkuk
- Zephaniah
- Haggai
- Zechariah
- Malachi

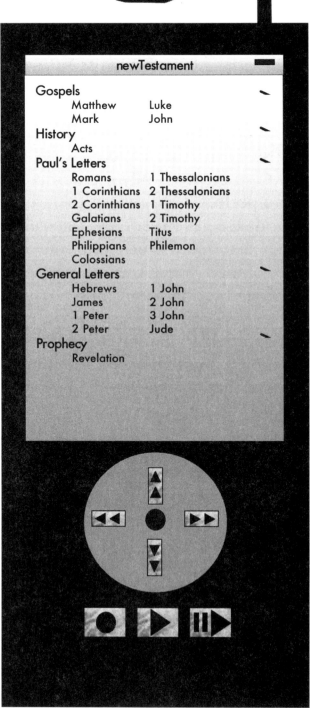

newTestament

Gospels
- Matthew
- Mark
- Luke
- John

History
- Acts

Paul's Letters
- Romans
- 1 Corinthians
- 2 Corinthians
- Galatians
- Ephesians
- Philippians
- Colossians
- 1 Thessalonians
- 2 Thessalonians
- 1 Timothy
- 2 Timothy
- Titus
- Philemon

General Letters
- Hebrews
- James
- 1 Peter
- 2 Peter
- 1 John
- 2 John
- 3 John
- Jude

Prophecy
- Revelation

myWord

Search

Source	Book	Division	Old or New Testament

Old Testament

- Law
- Old Testament History
- Poetry
- Major Prophets
- Minor Prophets

New Testament

- Gospels
- New Testament History
- Paul's Letters
- General Letters
- Prophecy

Book	Division	Old or New Testament
ex: Genesis	Law	Old
Job		
E _ _ e _ _ _ n _	Paul's Letters	
H _ s e _		Old
M _ _ t h _ _		
_ e v e _ _ t _ _ _	Prophecy	
Exodus		
_ _ t h	OT History	
R _ m _ _ _	Paul's Letters	
Isaiah		
_ _ k e		New
P s _ _ _ _	Poetry	
_ e r e m _ _ _	Major Prophets	
1 _ e t _ _		New
O _ _ d _ a h		Old
2 Samuel		
A _ t _		New
G _ _ _ _ t _ a n s		New
_ e b r _ w _	General Letters	
_ a b a _ _ _ _	Minor Prophets	

Session 2 Activity 1

7

HE'S NOT HERE!

MATTHEW 28:5–6

"Don't be afraid! I know you're looking for Jesus, who was crucified. He's not here. He has been brought back to life as he said."

MARK 16: 6

"Don't panic! You're looking for Jesus from Nazareth, who was crucified. He has been brought back to life. He's not here."

LUKE 24:5–6

"Why are you looking among the dead for the living one? He's not here. He has been brought back to life!"

Decode the Scroll

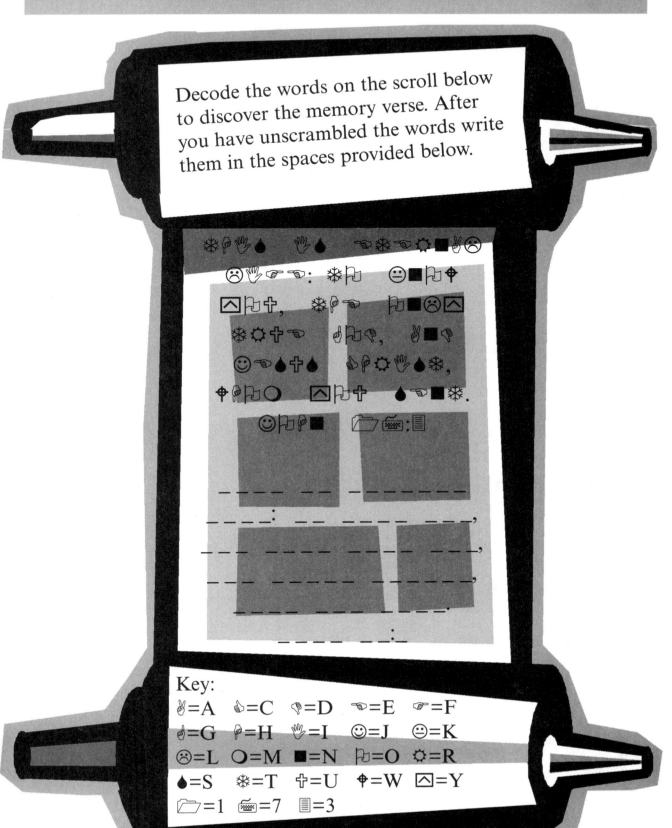

Decode the words on the scroll below to discover the memory verse. After you have unscrambled the words write them in the spaces provided below.

Key:
- ✌=A 👍=C 👎=D 👉=E 👉=F
- ☝=G 🖐=H 🖐=I ☺=J 😐=K
- 😞=L ○=M ■=N 👌=O ✿=R
- ♦=S ❄=T ✝=U ⚜=W ⬓=Y
- 🗁=1 ⌨=7 📄=3

GOD PROTECTED HIS MESSAGE

[Jesus said], "I assure you, until heaven and earth disappear, even the smallest detail of God's law will remain until its purpose is achieved." Matthew 5:18, NLT

The Bible we have today is the same message that God gave to people in Bible times because God protected his Word.

King Josiah was only eight years old when he began to rule the Israelites. He loved God. Kings who did not obey God let the temple become ruins. While restoring the temple, the scrolls of God's laws were found. They were safe all along. God knew where they were because God was protecting his Word.

> **Big Truth:**
> God protected his message through history so we could know what he is like.

God used careful scribes to make hundreds of copies of the Old Testament. God used a group of people called the Essenes to copy and hide many Old Testament scrolls in caves on the west side of the Dead Sea. These copies of the Old Testament were hidden for more than 2,000 years. All along God knew where they were because he was protecting his Word.

God guided the first Christians to take care of the New Testament. In early New Testament days the Roman government ordered Christians to stop their work and destroy their books. Many believers were placed in prison and killed because they chose to protect God's Word. Our Bible can be trusted to be true because God has always protected his Word.

The Dead Sea Scroll

1. What are they?
223 copies of manuscripts of the Old Testament.

2. When and where were they found?
They were discovered in 1947 in caves on the west side of the Dead Sea.

3. When were they written/copied?
They were written or copied about 125 years before Jesus was born.

4. The Exciting News!
After they were translated, they had the same message we can find in the Old Testament of our Bible.

God took care of his Word so we could know him.

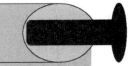

Scribe Rules

1. You may not copy from your memory. You must look at every letter. Example: If you want to write the word PRAY, copy letter-for-letter, like: p-p, r-r, a-a, y-y. Look at every letter before and after you copy it.

2. Count the number of times each letter of the alphabet occurs in the page you are copying. (Scribes had to count the number of times each letter of the alphabet occurred in each book!) Compare it to the original from which you are copying.

3. Each line you write out has to be exactly the same length as the original line you are copying.

4. Letters cannot touch each other. There has to be a space between them.

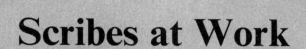

Scribes at Work

Scribe, copy Matthew 5:18 using the Scribe's Rules.

I assure you, until heaven and earth disappear, even the smallest detail of God's law will remain until its purpose is achieved.

Matthew 5:18, NLT

_____

_____

_____

_____

Instructions: Complete the crossword puzzle, then write the completed memory verse in the space provided below.

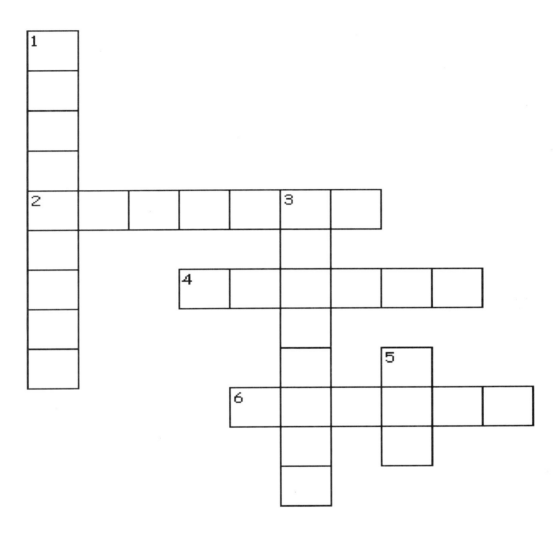

Down
1. and earth _____,
3. even the _____ detail
5. of God's _____

Across
2. until its _____ is achieved.
4. I assure you, until _____
6. will _____

Write the verse in correct order:

_____

_____

_____

THE BIBLE SHOWS US WHAT JESUS IS LIKE

"Imitate God, since you are the children he loves." Ephesians 5:1

In our Bible study the last three weeks, we have learned that the Bible is a Holy Book written by God. God gave us the Bible because he wanted us to get to know him. God has carefully protected his message through all the years in history. All three of those lessons are important to the next big truth which is that the Bible is really all about Jesus. If we want to live a life that is pleasing to God, we must live and love like Jesus did.

There are many fantastic Bible stories about Jesus. Jesus was a teacher. He healed people of all sorts of illnesses and problems. He could bless a little boy's lunch and feed 5,000 people. He could calm a storm in the Sea of Galilee by speaking to the winds and waves. All these miraculous things teach us that Jesus is God.

> **Big Truth:**
> The Bible gives us a perfect picture of what Jesus is like so that we can know how to be like him.

Each Bible story about Jesus tells us what he was really like. We should want to be like him. Today we are going to look closely at the night Jesus was having the Passover supper for the last time on earth with his disciples. He did an amazing thing to show his love for them. Jesus washed their feet! He took on the role of a servant and showed them he loved them.

What Jesus is Like

Think about what the following Bible stories tell us about Jesus' character.
Some suggested answers are: merciful, powerful, without sin,
God, compassionate.

Bible Story:
Jesus heals a paralytic.
Jesus is _____
Matthew 9:1–8

Bible Story:
Jesus pays the Temple tax.
Jesus is _____
Matthew 14:24–26

Bible Story:
Jesus walks on water.
Jesus is _____
Matthew 14:22–36

Bible Story:
Jesus and the woman at the well.
Jesus is _____
John 4:4–26

Bible Story:
Jesus feeds the 5000.
Jesus is _____
Matthew 14:13–18

Bible Story:
Jesus teaches the people.
Jesus is _____
Matthew 5

I Can Choose to Be Like Jesus

Jesus answered him, "'Love the Lord your God with all your heart, with all your soul, and with all your mind.' This is the greatest and most important commandment. The second is like it: 'Love your neighbor as you love yourself.'" Matthew 22:37–39

How can I live what this verse tells me to do in these four places? Write your answers in the squares below.

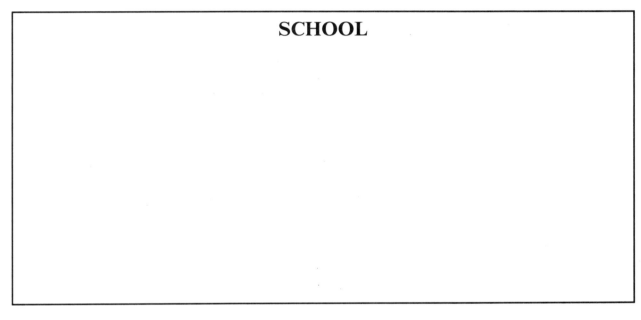

SCHOOL

PLAYGROUND / SPORTS TEAM

HOME

CHURCH

Instructions: Decode the puzzle below by finding the number that goes with each letter and filling in the blanks below to reveal our Bible memory verse.

Note: Not all of the letters will be used.

A	B	C	D	E	F	G	H	I	J	K	L	M	N	O	P	Q	R	S	T	U	V	W	X	Y	Z
15		8	17	4	22		14				26	25	11		10		20		24		1	19			

```
"  _ _ T A T E  G O _ ,  _ N C E  Y O _  A R E
   13 21 13 20 15 20 17  4 25 18  3 13 26 8 17  19 25 7  15 10 17

 T H E  C H _ _ R E N  H E _ O V E _ .  _ V E
 20 22 17  8 22 13 5 18 10 17 26  22 17 5 25 24 17 3   5 13 24 17

 _ N _ O V E _ A _  C H R _ _ T _ A _ O  O V E _
 13 26 5 25 24 17  15 3  8 22 10 13 3 20 15 5 3 25  5 25 24 17 18

   _ _ .  H E  G A V E  H _ _  _ E _ _ _  _ O R  _ _
   7 3    22 17  4 15 24 17  22 13 3   5 13 2 17   2 25 10  7 3

 A _  A N _ O _  _ E R _ N G _ A N _  _ A C R _ _ _ C E ,
 15 3  15 26 25 2  2 17 10 13 26 4  15 26 18  3 15 8 10 13 2 13 8 17

   A _  _ O O T H _ N G  A R O _ A  T O  G O _ . "
   15   3 25 25 20 22 13 26 4  15 10 25 21 15  20 25  4 25 18
```

THE HOLY SPIRIT—GOD'S GIFT TO US

But when the Holy Spirit controls our lives, he will produce this kind of fruit in us: love, joy, peace, patience, kindness, goodness, faithfulness, gentleness, and self-control.
Galatians 5:22–23, NLT

During the Last Supper Jesus had with all his disciples, he took time to prepare them for what was about to happen. Jesus knew that soon he would be arrested; he would die on a cross, rise again because he is God, and ascend into heaven. He did not want the disciples to feel abandoned when they could no longer see him daily. So he told the disciples that God had a plan to send them a helper. The helper is the Holy Spirit.

John, the beloved disciple, recorded Jesus' teachings about the Holy Spirit in the 14th to 17th chapters of John. The Holy Spirit is the third Person of the Trinity. When we say that God is a Trinity, we mean that we believe in one God who relates to us in three wonderful ways. We believe in God the Father, who desires to protect and provide for us. We believe in God the Son, whom we call Jesus Christ who is the Savior of our sins. We believe in God the Holy Spirit who becomes a part of each believer in Jesus. The Holy Spirit teaches and guides us.

> **Big Truth:**
> When Jesus went to heaven the Holy Spirit was sent to teach us how to live and love others the way Jesus loves them.

As the Holy Spirit works in our life, his fruit will be visible in our behaviors. He will take our impatience and replace it with his patience and so on until all the fruit of the Spirit is visible in our life, and we look more like Jesus.

Jesus Teaches His Disciples
about the Holy Spirit

Jesus said: "If you love me, you will obey my commandments. I will ask the Father, and he will give you another helper who will be with you forever. That helper is the Spirit of Truth. The world cannot accept him, because it doesn't see or know him. You know him, because he lives with you and will be in you" (John 14:15–17).

"I have told you this while I'm still with you. However, the helper, the Holy Spirit, whom the Father will send in my name, will teach you everything. He will remind you of everything that I have ever told you" (John 14:25–26).

"The helper whom I will send to you from the Father will come. This helper, the Spirit of Truth who comes from the Father, will declare the truth about me" (John 15:26).

"However, I am telling you the truth: It's good for you that I'm going away. If I don't go away, the helper won't come to you. But if I go, I will send him to you. He will come to convict the world of sin, to show the world what has God's approval, and to convince the world that God judges it. He will convict the world of sin, because people don't believe in me. He will show the world what has God's approval, because I'm going to the Father and you won't see me anymore" (John 16:7–10).

"When the Spirit of Truth comes, he will guide you into the full truth. He won't speak on his own. He will speak what he hears and will tell you about things to come. He will give me glory, because he will tell you what I say. Everything the Father says is also what I say, 'He will take what I say and tell it to you'" (John 16:13–15).

THE HOLY SPIRIT IS MY HELPER

Instructions: Draw a picture of one way God's Holy Spirit can help you.

The Ultimate Transformer Match Up

We Can Naturally Be:	The Holy Spirit Can Provide Us With:
Selfish	Joy
Hateful	Self-Control
Sad	Faithfulness
Worried	Patience
Impatient	Kindness
Mean	Peace
Bad	Love
Cruel	Goodness
Undisciplined	Gentleness

THE FRUITS OF THE SPIRIT

Instructions: The Fruits of the Spirit are LOVE, JOY, PEACE, PATIENCE, KINDNESS, GOODNESS, FAITHFULNESS, GENTLE-NESS, and SELF-CONTROL. Begin the maze at the "start" sign and work your way through, avoiding the other "fruit," to make it to the Bible where the real Fruits of the Spirit can be found.

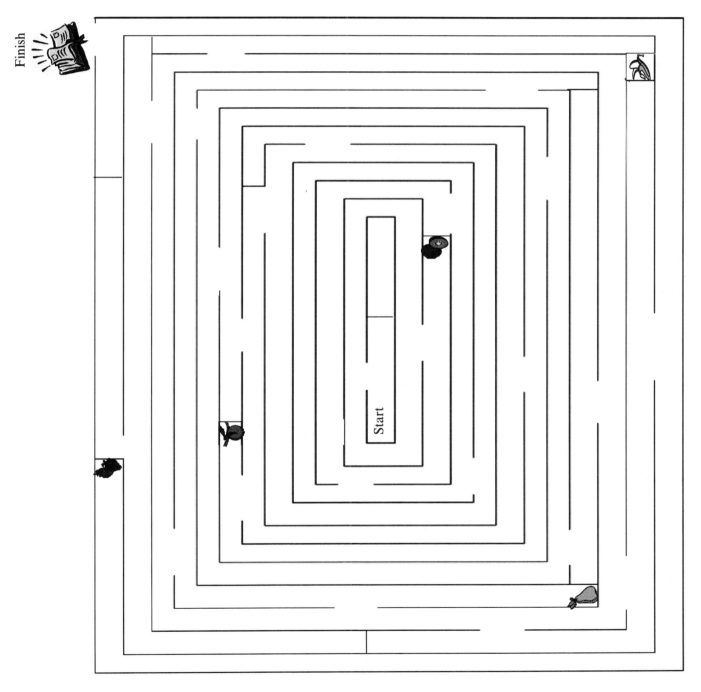

SELFISHNESS KEEPS ME FROM LOVING LIKE JESUS

*I'm giving you a new commandment: Love each other
in the same way that I have loved you.* John 13:34

God created us with the ability to have a friendship with him and with other people. When we decide to live our life just to make ourselves happy, we are not pleasing God. God does not want us to be selfish.

Jesus spent his life caring for others. So if we truly want to follow him we will need to put our selfishness aside and choose to care for people in the way that Jesus loves and cares for them. The good news is that the Holy Spirit will give us the power to live in a way that pleases God. The more we experience the love of Jesus, the more the Holy Spirit will cause us to want to be just like him.

Big Truth:

Letting go of selfishness and depending on Jesus will help you to love like Jesus loves.

One day Jesus and the disciples were walking toward Capernaum. Jesus could hear the disciples arguing. He asked them what they were arguing about. They were silent. They had been arguing about which one of them was the greatest and best. They were being selfish. Jesus told them that to be the most important person, they had to be willing to be the servant of others.

Naomi was a widow. She lived in a foreign land with her two daughters-in-law. When she heard there was food again in her home city of Bethlehem, she wanted to go back there. She told her two daughters-in-law to go back to their parents' homes and marry again. One daughter-in-law did just that. But Ruth would not leave Naomi all alone in her old age. Ruth is an example of a person who was not selfish. God later blessed Ruth with a family in Bethlehem.

Just the way kids are. . . But does it please God?

Read the following case studies and think through the questions at the end.

Case 1—Teasing hurts!

Bruce was a good kid. He got along great with his parents and most kids and was an *A/B* student. There were two boys, Carlos and Nicolas, whom he really wanted as best friends. They were very popular and smart. They only made *A's*. They teased him whenever he was the last one to turn in his paper in class. They teased him in P.E. by saying he ran like a girl. They made all the other children in class laugh at him too. Bruce often felt bad inside; even though his parents were happy with his grades, he was not happy because he felt embarrassed by being teased by Carlos and Nicolas. Bruce kept doing everything he could to get Carlos and Nicolas to like him. What more could he do?

1. Who was acting in an unloving way? _____

2. Bullies sometimes use words instead of fists. A person who picks on or teases another person all the time is a bully even if he or she never hits anyone. Name some choices Bruce could make. (There could be many.)

   a. _____

   _____

   b. _____

   _____

3. How can you choose to please God in response to someone who is teasing you?

   _____

   _____

   _____

   _____

Think: If God were writing the end of this story, what would it say?

Case 2—What to do with Skittles

Kristen and Collin are sister and brother. They usually get along. One Saturday afternoon they were having a great time watching a movie. Collin remembered that he had a whole bag of Skittles in his backpack. He went and got it. Kristen saw the bag of Skittles and asked Collin to share. Collin said, "No, they are mine, and I don't have to share everything!"

1. Who was acting in an unloving way?

   _____

2. What are Kristen's choices?

   _____

   _____

   _____

   _____

3. What are Collin's choices?

   _____

   _____

   _____

   _____

Think: If God were writing the end of this story, what would it say?

COMMANDED TO LOVE OTHERS

Instructions: Search out where in the Scriptures these commands are given. One will be used twice.

1. Love each other. _____

2. Be devoted to each other like a loving family. _____

3. Show respect for each other. _____

4. Live in harmony with each other. _____

5. Accept each other. _____

6. Serve each other through love. _____

SCRIPTURE BOX

Galatians 5:13	1 John 3:11	Romans 12:10
Ephesians 4:2	Romans 15:7	Romans 12:16

MirroregamI

Try to break the code below. Write down what you think the answer is in the space provided. After you have written it down, look at the original message in a mirror to see if you guessed right.

wen a uoy gnivig m'I"
evol: tnemdnammoc
eht ni rehto hcae
I taht yaw emas
".uoy devol evah
TWG 43:31 nhoJ

_____

_____

_____

_____

We are to be mirror images of Christ!

FOLLOWING JESUS' EXAMPLE GIVES ME JOY

The LORD wants you to obey his commands and laws that I'm giving you today for your own good . . . You'll be blessed if you obey the commands of the LORD your God. Deuteronomy 10:13, 11:27

Everyone wants to be happy. Happy is a feeling that can come and go. God has planned that we could experience real joy in our heart no matter what is going on in our world. Joy comes in obeying the commandments and laws God has given us. So how does obedience lead to happiness and joy?

When we love others like Jesus loves people, we will treat them with respect and have better relationships with people. Having right relationships with people results in real joy in our life. When we do not treat others in ways that are kind and fair, we will have strife. When we make the right choices and are kind and loving to other people, we will receive more love and care from them.

> **Big Truth:**
> The more I love people like Jesus loves them, the more joy I will have.

At times you will care for others, and they will never thank you. You can still feel the joy in your heart if what you did was first to obey God's commands to love others. Obeying God always results in benefits for your own good, as our Bible verse says.

When we follow the **STEPS OF TRUTH** to make the right choices, especially in our friendships with others, we will be blessed with God's protection even if the choice was hard. We can also count on God to provide what we need. The **STEPS OF TRUTH** are:

Consider the choice. The Bible teaches us what is right and wrong. Ask yourself: What will happen if I choose to do what I am thinking about?

Compare it to God. The Bible teaches us what God is like. Ask yourself: Does what I want to do reflect God's nature? The Bible teaches us that God is love, so if I want to hurt another person, I will know it is the wrong choice.

Commit to God's way. The next step is to decide to do the right thing even if it is going to be hard to do, or if I will be unpopular for doing the right thing.

Count on God's protection and provision. Once I do the right thing, I can know that God will protect me and he will provide what I really need. I will be blessed for making the right choice.

THE STEPS OF TRUTH

Choosing to be honest is for my own good.

Give an example of a time when you are tempted to lie, cheat, or steal.

_____

_____

CONSIDER THE CHOICE—How can you decide what is right?

List the benefits and consequences of your choices.

If I choose _____   If I choose _____
        (to do what is wrong)   *(to do what is right)*

The benefits are	*The consequences are*	*The benefits are*	*The consequences are*
_____	_____	_____	_____
_____	_____	_____	_____
_____	_____	_____	_____

COMPARE IT TO GOD—What does God say? "Do not steal. Do not lie. Do not deceive one another" (Leviticus 19:11).

God is True

COMMIT TO GOD'S WAY—How can you choose to obey God in the situation about which you wrote?

_____

COUNT ON GOD'S PROTECTION AND PROVISION—How can choosing God's way protect and provide for us?

☑Check the benefits you get from your specific right choice

God Protects Me from
- ☐ guilt
- ☐ shame
- ☐ cycle of deceit
- ☐ ruined relationships

God Provides Me with
- ☐ clear conscience
- ☐ sense of accomplishment
- ☐ good reputation
- ☐ trusting relationships